Cast Iron
and the
Crescent City

Ann M. Masson *and* Lydia H. Schmalz

Cast Iron and the Crescent City

Ann M. Masson *and* Lydia H. Schmalz

A Louisiana Landmarks Society Book

PELICAN PUBLISHING COMPANY
Gretna 2012

Copyright © 1995 by Louisiana Landmarks Society
All rights reserved

Published by arrangement with the Louisiana Landmarks
Society by Pelican Publishing Company, Inc., 2012

First printing, 1995
First Pelican edition, 2012

*The word "Pelican" and the depiction of a pelican are trademarks
of Pelican Publishing Company, Inc., and are registered in the U.S.
Patent and Trademark Office.*

Library of Congress Catalog Card Number: 95-80470
ISBN: 9781589809949

Photographs by Frank W. Masson and Ann M. Masson

Printed in the United States of America
Published by Pelican Publishing Company, Inc.
1000 Burmaster Street, Gretna, Louisiana 70053

The ironwork of the French Quarter is familiar to all who know New Orleans. Much of this is cast iron made in New Orleans and other cities during the 19th century. The balconies and verandahs of the French Quarter are but one use of the popular building material and are the products of a thriving business which supported many residents of the Crescent City.

Mass-production methods developed for casting iron made it a favorite material for use in buildings, machines, and tools in the 19th century. The development of the iron industry at that time was rapid, contributing to and profiting from the technological progress of other industries. By mid-century, decorative and structural cast iron was widely used as a building material, partially replacing wood, wrought iron, and other materials. Many utilitarian objects were produced for the home including stoves, garden furniture, cooking implements, irons, holloware, tools, and hardware. Cast-iron fences, statuary, fountains, and vases were widely available. Most important to technological progress was the manufacture of heavy machinery, steam engines, components for bridges and large buildings, and transportation equipment. Advances in foundry techniques made possible the production of these large, complicated items so essential to the economic growth of industrialized nations. In his book, *The Founding of Metals* (1877), foundryman Edward Kirk expressed the opinion of many Victorians:

> Iron has come into such general use in modern times that the development of the iron resources of a country may readily indicate the advancement of a nation; for iron has become the symbol of civilization; its value in the arts can be measured only by the progress of the present age, in its adaptation to the useful arts; it has kept pace with the scientific discoveries and improvements, so that the uses of iron have become universal; it is worth more to the world than all the other metals combined.

According to William Fairbairn, noted student of the iron industry, cast iron was first used in quantity in 1543 when a number of cannons were made in Sussex, England. By the early 1700s, the Coalbrookdale Ironworks was in operation, a firm whose leadership continued well into the 19th century. During the 18th century, experiments were made with equipment, fuels, and ores and by 1750, coke, prepared by reducing coal, was introduced to replace charcoal as a fuel for blast furnaces. Attempts were made in England to use cast iron in the construction of machinery. The first bridge using the new material was constructed in 1773 near Coalbrookdale. William Fairbairn, in his book *On the Application of Cast and Wrought Iron to Building Purposes* (1854), comments on the early use of structural cast iron in buildings:

> The first instance on record of the successful application of cast-iron beams to the purposes of building, is that of a fire-proof cotton-mill erected by Messrs. Phillips and Lee of Manchester. This mill was built in the year 1801...From 1801 till 1824 little or no variation took place in the form of beams, and for a quarter of a century Messrs. Phillips and Lee's mill offered the model for similar buildings.

In 1824 an Englishman, Nielson, received a patent on the hot-blast process, which revolutionized the iron industry. Previously, blasts, or streams of cold air, were used to fan the fuel in the furnace. The hot blast, achieved by preheating the air in an auxiliary chamber, created a hotter fire and allowed the use of coal as a fuel. The increase in the quality of pig iron was minimal, but the increase in quantity was enormous. More iron could be processed at a time, and more cheaply, through the use of the hot blast. Steady demand for the improved product prompted foundrymen to develop better techniques, more scientific methods, and new applications. By the 1830s the cast-iron industry in England was developing rapidly. The catalog of the Crystal Palace Exhibition reported in 1851 that the annual production of iron in Great Britain was upwards of 2,250,000 tons.

American cast-iron production was greatly influenced by English technological advances. Although the adoption of new processes required considerable capital expenditure, American manufacturers began using the hot-blast process and mineral fuel. The production of pig iron increased, and by the 1850s large American cities had foundries capable of converting the pigs into useful and decorative objects.

Companies in New York, Philadelphia, and Baltimore were the leaders of the industry and many of their products were shipped to other cities. Their designs, circulated by catalog, were copied and their innovative ideas were used by other founders. Some Eastern firms had branch offices in other cities. In New Orleans, Wood, Miltenberger & Co. represented the Philadelphia firm of Wood & Perot. Local newspapers contain advertisements from companies in New York, New Jersey, Kentucky, and Alabama. Trade catalogs, so instrumental in spreading pattern designs, were produced by the most successful firms as advertising for their standardized items. Often catalogs listed prices as well as the most notable uses of their products. The ironwork catalogs of the Architectural Iron Works of the City of New York (D. D. Badger, pres.), the New York Wire Railing Company (Hutchinson and Wickersham), and the Philadelphia Architectural Iron Company mention their important jobs in New Orleans. American, English, and French catalogs were widely circulated and influenced foundrymen throughout the country. Some designs appear in more than one catalog and their widespread use indicates that these elements were not exclusively produced by the originating company. Unless marked or authenticated by records, it is impossible to be certain which company produced a cast-iron object.

The cast-iron industry in New Orleans began with the

establishment of the Leeds Iron Foundry in 1825. The industry expanded during the following decades and reached its peak just before the Civil War. Advertisements in local newspapers indicate that quantities of pig iron, from which any article could be cast, were entering the city regularly. An 1851 notice announces the arrival of 500 tons; another in 1858 advertises 300 tons of "Scotch Pig Iron." Such shipments were not unusual and illustrate the quantity of cast-iron objects being produced in New Orleans. Many local companies specialized in the manufacture of sugar mill equipment and other machinery, advertising architectural elements as a sideline. Other companies were chiefly occupied with architectural production. In addition to foundries, there were numerous companies advertising as manufacturers of iron, blacksmiths, sheet-iron workers, and dealers in stoves and iron. City directories of the 1850s list hundreds of ironworkers, including blacksmiths, pattern makers, moulders, and founders. Census listings show that many New Orleans ironworkers were recent immigrants from Ireland and Germany. In 1860 other ironworkers were listed as free men of color, while a number were from England or other areas of the United States.

Most of the architectural ironwork produced in New Orleans was used decoratively, rather than for structural purposes. Architectural cast iron was used in New Orleans by the 1830s in combination with wrought iron. Small decorative castings were incorporated into wrought-iron fences and railings. The use of cast iron was furthered by the long tradition of ornamental ironwork in New Orleans. Residents were especially receptive to the new material and used it to replace earlier wrought-iron decoration. Ornamental cast iron was most popular during the 1850s, a period of growth and prosperity in New Orleans. Many large homes and new commercial structures built at that time were enhanced by the fashionable material. The *Daily Picayune*, July 7, 1852, contains the following comment: " One of the most admirable innovations upon the old system of building tall, staring structures for business purposes, is the plan which we are glad to see is generally coming in use, of erecting galleries and verandahs of ornamental iron work." Although many 19th century writers favored cast-iron ornament, some architects disagreed because they found too much of the decorative material aesthetically unappealing.

Research indicates that much New Orleans ironwork was painted a bronze color or a soft, bright green. Several building contracts specify that cast-iron verandahs be painted bronze. The contracts for the fences at Jackson Square and Washington Square indicate that bronze paint was to be used. Archaeological investigation at the Pontalba Buildings has recently revealed a paint color which may be the bronze specified in building contracts. Many architectural drawings show a soft green on verandahs, fences, and balconies. Some iron fences were polychromed in naturalistic colors, while cast-iron building fronts were generally painted in imitation of stone.

The large-scale production of ornamental cast iron was interrupted by the Civil War when many foundries began manufacturing war materiel. The *Daily Delta*, March 3, 1862, comments on Bennett & Lurges, a foundry greatly affected by the Civil War: "From such works as casting and building the Free Market, their attention has been directed to the preparation of munitions of war, and now you will see in their extensive establishment any quantity of shot and shell." Although some decorative elements and building fronts were made in New Orleans during the late 1860s, depressed economic conditions reduced the output of many foundries. Some firms failed and others turned to the production of machinery. By the last quarter of the century, renewed prosperity encouraged the opening of new foundries. However, public taste had changed and ornamental cast iron was no longer in such great demand. Steel began to replace iron in many phases of manufacturing and construction. Some New Orleans foundries remained in business well into the 20th century, but never produced in quantity the ornamental ironwork so popular in the 1850s.

New Orleans is fortunate to have retained so much of its decorative cast iron, now lost in many other cities. A growing awareness of our architectural heritage should make possible the continued preservation of these superb examples of 19th century taste.

The differences between wrought iron and cast iron are caused by a variance in carbon content. Wrought iron contains approximately .04 percent carbon while cast iron contains from 2 percent to 6 percent carbon. Wrought iron is a malleable substance which may be shaped by hammering, stretching, or rolling. Available in bars, rods, and plates, wrought iron is made into decorative forms by individual craftsmen who form the heated iron on an anvil. The final product is strong and very dense. Wrought iron is most suited to geometric or curvilinear designs which reflect the form of the original material. Wrought iron may be waxed for protection as it is quite resistant to rust.

Cast iron is a brittle substance which fractures easily upon impact. The material, available in pigs, is melted in a furnace and the molten iron poured into a prepared mould. After cooling and finishing, the product is ready for use. Cast iron is suitable for many designs, especially the complex and naturalistic patterns popular with the Victorians. Many pieces can be cast from the same pattern and repetitive designs are easily manufactured. Cast iron can usually be recognized by its poured or moulded appearance, and by its rough surface on unfinished interior parts. The product is more susceptible to rust than wrought iron and should be painted for protection.

A number of books were published during the 19th century to instruct foundrymen and provide technical information on iron ores, pattern making, finishing, new equipment, and methods of production. During the 19th century, most iron was smelted from its ores in blast furnaces located near the sources of ore and fuel. The largest class of furnaces in the 1850s produced from 120 to 160 tons a week. The hot-blast furnace, using anthracite coal as fuel, was widely used, producing an economical iron suitable for light castings. As the iron was smelted from its ores, it flowed to the bottom of the furnace and out through channels cut in the sand floor. From the main channel, where it was known as the sow-pig, the iron flowed into moulds, or pigs. The final product, called pig iron or cast iron, was removed from the mould and shipped to foundries which re-melted the iron and cast it into the desired shape. The iron could also be cast directly from the furnace. The manufacture of pig iron was a large industry centered in Pennsylvania and the Ohio River Valley. There were numerous grades of pig iron determined by the chemical content, the kinds of ores and fuels used, and the process by which it was smelted. In 1885 Thomas D. West wrote in his book *American Foundry Practice:*

Twenty-five or thirty years ago pig iron was not so easily procured as at the present day; much of the iron used was imported, and what few brands of iron were in the market were generally well known. At the present day, however, we find the home production so large that it would occupy pages to even mention the different kinds, and the importations are so small that we seldom hear of any.

When the pig iron reached its destination, it was again melted, at from 2000 degrees to 3000 degrees, and poured into moulds prepared from laboriously carved patterns. Skilled pattern makers were essential to the operation of a successful foundry. The pattern maker's task, combining the skills of a joiner and turner, was to carve a wooden pattern of the design. Pine and mahogany were the best woods for most patterns, although other woods were used for special purposes. Smooth, straight-grained, well-seasoned wood insured a good pattern that, with proper care and storage, could be used repeatedly. Patterns were treated with various substances to make them draw more easily from the sand. Treatment depended on the type of wood, the size and complexity of the pattern, and how often the pattern had been used. Other materials, such as cast iron, brass, zinc, plaster of Paris, wax, and glass, were occasionally used to make patterns. If a pattern was needed for repetitive castings, a cast-iron pattern, more durable than wood, was usually made. Iron tended to shrink in casting, sometimes as much as a quarter of an inch to the foot, and patterns were designed to compensate for this. According to Edward Kirk, *The Founding of Metals* (1885), "The average shrinkage always counted on in making patterns, is one eighth of an inch to the foot."

After the pattern was completed, the moulder's work began. The moulder packed the pattern in the appropriate medium, usually sand, and designed the vents which allowed the escape of gas when the mould was poured. Each mould required one or more gates, the openings through which the iron was poured, and the moulder was responsible for the positioning of these channels. The pattern was removed, leaving an accurate impression of the design in the moulding material. The mould was further prepared by tightly packing the sand and dusting it with coal dust or other substances, which resisted the intrusion of the iron into the moulding material. The molten iron was poured into the mould and allowed to cool completely. Castings were removed from the mould and smoothed with files, grindstones, or emery wheels before they were assembled into the final product. The moulder's skill was essential. A number of choices had to be made to insure a good casting, including the type of moulding material, the location of vents and gates, and the state of the iron when poured. Books of the 19th century recommended apprenticeship training for moulders and stressed that few moulders were skilled at all types of casting.

The size of a foundry, its structure, and the variety of materials and craftsmen necessary to the operation depended, during the 19th century, on what type of work was being done. Thomas D. West, *American Foundry Practice* (1885), commented:

> Shops that do heavy and light work should have the light work done in parts of the shop entirely separated from the heavy floors, for the reason that grades of sand better adapted for each class of work can then be used, and the work done to pay better. The portion of the building to be used for moulding of heavy castings should be constructed with a view to strength, while the portion for the light casting can be constructed more cheaply.

From this and other descriptions, it is evident that foundries were often large establishments, sometimes requiring a city block to accommodate their numerous departments. In 1888 *New Orleans and the New South* gave this description of H. Dudley Coleman & Co.'s facilities:

> The works include departments as follows: Carpenter shop, blacksmith shops, moulding floors, pattern shop, mill shop, machine shops, shops for sheet-iron work, etc., and to these will shortly be added a boiler shop.

EDWARDS & HAUBTMAN.

From *New Orleans and the New South* (1888).

Hinderer's Iron Works, 1780 Prytania Street.

Mechanics' Institute, from Jewell's *Crescent City Illustrated* (1873). (Courtesy of Koch and Wilson Architects)

This brick building, stuccoed and painted in imitation of granite, was built by the New Orleans Mechanics' Society after the original institute burned in 1854. The architect was James Gallier, Jr. Described by J. Curtis Waldo in 1879 as "substantial and stately," the Mechanics' Institute was located on the east side of Dryades Street near Canal. On the lower floor were the library and committee room of the New Orleans Mechanics' Society. Other areas of the large building were occupied by state offices, including the Hall of the Louisiana House of Representatives. The Society was organized in 1806 and had as projects the operation of a public library and the education of tradesmen. A constitution adopted in 1855 states that the organization consisted of mechanics, manufacturers, and artists of New Orleans and its suburbs. In 1870 over 250 members were active in the Mechanics' Society, whose facilities provided a meeting place for prominent New Orleans businessmen, including those involved in iron founding. Among the officers in 1872 were Luther Homes, John A. Shakespeare, and James D. Edwards, proprietors of local foundries.

622 Canal Street.

The Sunday edition of the *Daily Picayune*, August 21, 1859, reported: "The cast-iron front of the Merchants' Insurance Company, on Canal Street, is nearly finished. These castings were made here, after the designs of our young fellow townsman, Mr. W. Freret, Jr., architect. It is a mixed style of architecture, highly ornamented, and the design, of a quite novel model, is very tasteful." This building was one of many cast-iron fronts erected in the Central Business District during the 1850s. Unfortunately, most have been destroyed. Designed to imitate stone, the fronts, cast both locally and in other cities, were based in concept on the buildings erected by Daniel Badger, president of the Architectural Iron Works of the City of New York. An 1865 catalog of this firm shows many designs for cast-iron buildings. In the introduction, it is stated that Mr. Badger erected in 1842 in Boston the first American cast-iron structure. Columns and lintels on the first floor were made of cast iron. The first building in the United States made entirely of cast iron was erected by James Bogardus in New York in 1848. As early structures proved durable and practical, more iron was used on commercial buildings. The Badger firm lists two cast-iron fronts they provided for New Orleans businessmen prior to 1865: for Paul Tulane, a 47 foot five-story front; for J. B. Lee, a 62 foot store front.

One of the most spectacular fronts in New Orleans was cast by Jones, McElvain & Co., Holly Springs, Mississippi, for J.C. Barelli between 1858 and 1860. Called the Moresque Building, the structure was unfinished for a number of years and finally occupied by the firm of John Gauche, importer of china and glassware. The three-story building, designed in the Moorish style by W. A. Freret and completed by James Freret, consisted of four elaborate fronts, each 150 feet long, erected at the corner of Camp and Poydras; it was destroyed by fire in 1897. Among the cast-iron fronts in New Orleans were: the Sidney Story Building, Canal between St. Charles and Camp, designed by Gallier and Turpin, 1853; Dr. Mackie's Stores, corner Camp and Common, designed by Reynolds, cast by Bottom and Tiffany's Celebrated Eagle Iron Works, Trenton, N.J., 1859; the New Orleans Savings Institution, corner Baronne and Canal, designed by W. A. Freret, cast by Leeds & Co., 1873; the Rice, Borne & Co. Building, Camp Street, cast by Reynolds Iron Works. All have been destroyed.

111 Exchange Place.

111 Exchange Place.

The building at 111 Exchange Place was constructed by Gallier and Esterbrook, Architects and Builders, for the Bank of America. This five-story store with a cast-iron front was built as rental property by the bank, which occupied the corner of Canal and Exchange Place. The building contract of May 25, 1866, includes specifications for remodeling the extant bank. Members of the Board of the Bank of America approved the plans and specifications submitted by James Gallier, Jr. in May 1866, and gave full power to a building committee with whom the contract was drawn. The contract specified that the store was to be built first so that business could be conducted there while alterations were being made to the bank. The section entitled "Iron Work" reads: "An ornamental Iron front, similar to that of C. Slocomb's store on Canal Street, shall be furnished by the Bank, at the building; to the contractors by the Building Committee of the Bank, and the contractors shall then take charge of the same and have it set up in the best and most secure manner..." The front was to be integrated with the brick walls by the means of iron anchor ties. Interior cast-iron columns helped support the upper floors. Although C. J. Leeds, of Leeds Iron Foundry, was a member of the building committee, notes on James Gallier, Jr.'s drawings indicate that the front was cast by another local firm, Bennett & Lurges. The elaborate building, in the popular Italian Renaissance style, was first rented to Charles Cavaroc Co., Importers.

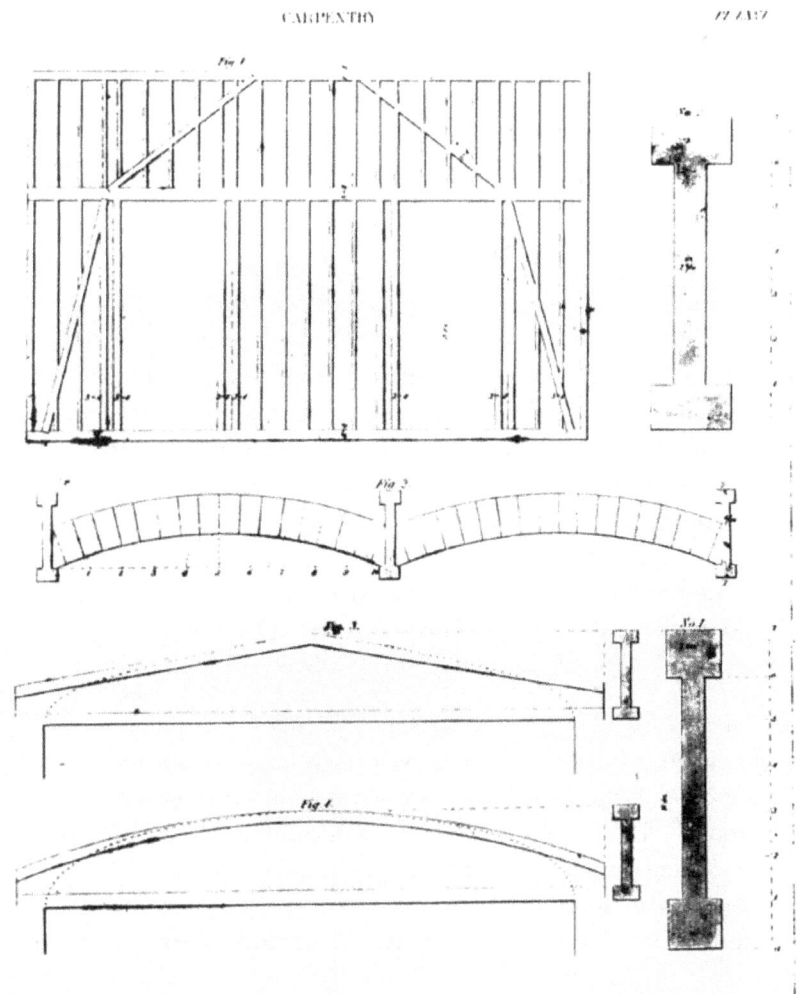

Illustration of the use of cast-iron beams, from *The Builder's Guide* (1850).

The value of cast iron as a structural building material was recognized during the 18th century, but it was not until the mid-19th century that its application was widespread. First used for bridges, beams, and girders, cast iron had limited success until foundry methods improved and the chance of faulty castings was minimized. The main building of the Crystal Palace Exhibition in London, 1851, designed by Sir John Paxton, was constructed primarily of iron and glass and greatly promoted structural applications. Cast-iron beams and girders were most used in factories and mills, where large spans were needed. They were also used in railway stations, warehouses, stores, foundries, and public buildings. Many structures in New Orleans had cast-iron beams, girders, or columns. The city waterworks was described in the *Daily Picayune*, July 24, 1864. The article illustrates the quantity of cast iron used in some structures:

> The foundation of the building is laid with granite, and the reservoir at the top, which will hold 175,000 gallons is supported by thirty-six cast iron columns, weighing 5,000 pounds each, with cornices and tablets at the top. The reservoir is reached by a spiral iron staircase, from the top of which a fine view of the river, and our great Canal street, is afforded. Besides the main pillars to support the great weight above, the inside also contains iron columns and beams, with a brick arched roof. The building is painted to represent brown stone, and the open iron filagree work greatly adds to the beauty of this fine edifice. The engines were built in St. Louis, and are already finished.

Castings for the large iron structure, intended to supply water for fire fighting and street cleaning, were made by the local firm, Bennett & Lurges. With the use of cast iron came the construction of fireproof buildings, built entirely of non-combustible materials and possessing a number of special safety features. This use of cast iron was relatively short-lived. The improved technology for producing steel soon made it the preferred material for structural purposes. The impact of the development of cast-iron structures should not be minimized, for in them lay the beginnings of the modern skyscraper and steel frame building.

The distinctive Gothic building at 923 Tchoupitoulas was designed by Gallier, Turpin & Co. as a store and warehouse for Leeds & Co., whose foundry was located at the corner of Foucher and Delord Streets. A James Gallier, Jr. drawing of this building is dated 1852. Another, dated March 1, 1850, shows a similar structure, but with four stories rather than three. This may have been an earlier scheme for the Leeds Store and Warehouse. As is typical of many commercial buildings, decorative cast iron appears on the facade in the form of columns, tie-ends, and ornamental window lintels. The warehouse is unusual in style, however, as most commercial structures were built in the Greek or Italianate styles. A column is marked "Leeds," indicating that the Leeds Foundry cast the ornamental ironwork for their building.

917-923 Tchoupitoulas Street.

The Pontalba Buildings flanking Jackson Square were built by Baroness Micaela Almonester de Pontalba as rental property containing stores and living space. James Gallier & Co., Architects, drew plans and elevations for the row houses and signed a building contract with the Baroness on May 30, 1849. There was subsequently a disagreement and Henry Howard, another local architect, was consulted. In *Jewell's Crescent City Illustrated* (1873), Howard takes credit for the design and superintendence of the work, although it is apparent that Baroness Pontalba maintained close supervision. She was responsible for many features of the buildings, including the design of the unusual cast-iron monogram "AP." The wood pattern for the monogram was carved by New Orleanian Waldemar Appolonius Talen. The full cast-iron verandah is probably the earliest in the city and was cast in New York. Recent archaeological investigation has revealed the original color of the ironwork, possibly the bronze color specified in building contracts of the mid-19th century.

The large house at the corner of Fourth and Prytania Streets was built in 1859 for Colonel Robert Henry Short. The architect was Henry Howard. In addition to ornamental cast-iron verandahs on the building, the property is surrounded by a distinctive cast-iron fence composed of cornstalks and morning glory vines. The fence, now a uniform green, was probably once painted in naturalistic colors as were others of its kind. A partially exposed maker's mark indicates that the fence was obtained from a local foundry, Wood, Miltenberger & Co., representatives of Wood & Perot, a successful Philadelphia firm. Quite possibly, the ironwork of the verandah, in a rose and geometric pattern, was obtained from the same firm. The extensive use of cast iron on the facade and the large fence is typical of Garden District homes.

500 block, St. Ann Street.

1448 Fourth Street.

1132 Royal Street. (Photograph by Frank Lotz Miller)

In 1857 James Gallier, Jr. purchased land at what is now 1132 Royal Street. By 1860, city directories list the Gallier family at this address, indicating that construction of the private residence had been completed. James Gallier, Jr. detailed his home in the popular Italianate style; the room arrangement is typical of mid-century New Orleans townhouses. The elaborate cast-iron verandah is supported by five cast-iron columns. The rose and tendril pattern of the verandah can be found on other New Orleans homes, but rarely has so complete an ensemble survived. Extensive repairs were made to the cornice, but all restoration was carefully matched to existing fragments. The elaborate cast-iron door grill is apparently unique in design.

A number of commercial buildings in the Central Business District, the Vieux Carre, and on Magazine Street have cast-iron square columns alternating with large doors or shop windows on the first level. Windows on the upper floors of these buildings are generally accented with cast-iron elements. The design of the capitals, often derived from Classical motifs, ranges from the simple Tuscan to the ornate Corinthian. Whether the iron of the columns is structural, or a purely decorative sheathing covering a brick support, is often difficult to determine. A building contract of April 7, 1852, between Thomas Hale, owner, and Henry Howard, architect, outlines the erection of four brick stores, situated within New Levee, Poydras, Fulton and Lafayette Streets. The section entitled "Iron Work" reads: "The fronts shall have cast iron story posts, lintels, and cornice finished according to the drawings and executed and set up in the most perfect and best substantial manner, the thickness of the castings to be at least one inch." During the mid-19th century, these durable first-floor fronts were quite fashionable, and the many identical ones were probably inexpensive, mass-produced items. Some are marked with the names of New Orleans foundries: Shakespeare Iron Foundry, St. Louis Street Foundry, Julia Street Foundry, and Bennett & Lurges. One is marked "Chickasaw Iron Works Memphis Tenn." The majority have no maker's marks and could have been manufactured by any of the numerous firms advertising their proficiency in this work.

1035 Decatur Street.

511 Decatur Street.

528 South Peters Street.

2805 Carondelet Street.

Purely decorative cast iron appears throughout the city on cottages, town houses, villas, and commercial buildings. Mid-century building contracts indicate that the term "verandah" frequently referred to the cast-iron structures used as auxiliary living spaces, generally on the front of buildings. The cast-iron verandah supported over the sidewalk by slender columns is most common in the Vieux Carre, while the multiple-story verandah is typical of the Garden District and other residential areas. Balconies, supported without columns or pillars, are smaller than verandahs and often replace earlier wrought-iron structures in the French Quarter. Cast-iron railings also ornament homes with wooden columns or turned posts. The extensive use of ornamental cast iron was most popular during the mid-19th century when many of New Orleans' fine homes were constructed. At this time, cast iron was sometimes added to the facades of existing buildings in an effort to keep in fashion. The manufacturing firm of Baumiller & Goodwyn, of New Orleans, added a cast-iron verandah and cornice to a building known as the Florence House, located at the southwest corner of South and Camp Streets. The building contract of 1854 indicates that verandah elements were ordered, by number, from the "Specimen Card" of Horton & Macy of Cincinnati, Ohio. The cornice was composed of a pattern known as "Baumiller & Goodwyn's dental [*sic*] cornice" combined with other elements ordered from Horton & Macy. Cast iron was more durable than wooden elements, cheaper than wrought iron, and could be purchased in a wide variety of patterns. Unfortunately, no maker's marks have been found on the delicate railings or their supports.

1410 Jackson Avenue.

WOOD & PEROT, PHILADELPHIA.
N° 369

WOOD & PEROT, PHILADELPHIA.
N° 370.

From *Designs of Ornamental Ironwork* (1860-61).

The variety of railing patterns available during the 19th century was enormous. An 1859 Wood, Miltenberger & Co. advertisement states that "200 varieties of Gallery Railings" and "50 [patterns] for verandahs" were available. Reflecting popular decorative and historical styles, railings could be purchased in Gothic, Classical, and geometric patterns. The naturalistic designs were perhaps most popular. Many railings are composed of roses, fuchsias and morning glories, acorns and oak leaves, fruit and trailing vines. Patterns were mixed and it is not unusual to find the same cast-iron elements combined in different ways. Some patterns can be found throughout the city while others are rare. Builders and homeowners selected cast-iron elements from catalogs or showrooms and the cheaper, mass-produced items were purchased most frequently. More expensive patterns were also made to an individual's specifications. Some railings and pattern designs were undoubtedly imported from the large foundries in Philadelphia and New York, but most were probably cast locally. City directories and census listings reveal that there were many pattern makers in New Orleans capable of carving the wood patterns and numerous foundries able to do the casting. Although the elements of verandahs were cast in foundries, they were probably assembled, with wrought iron structural members, by those who advertised themselves as "manufacturers" or "house smiths."

729 Camp Street.

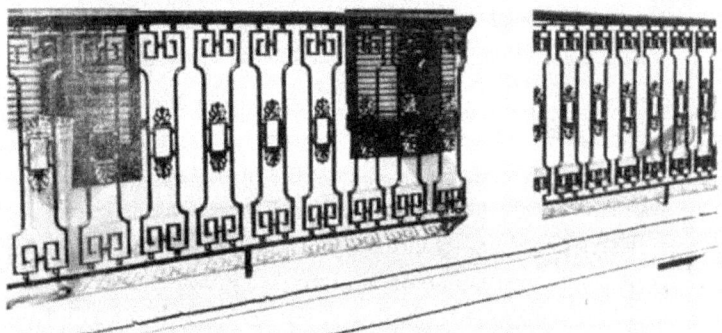

1450 Jackson Avenue.

1122-1124 Felicity Street.

500 block, St. Ann Street.

540 Royal Street.

1138 Washington Avenue.

300 St. Charles Avenue.

637 Common Street.

1100 Jackson Avenue.

917-923 Tchoupitoulas Street.

Decorative cast-iron elements above windows are called "window lintels" in the catalogs of two New York firms: the New York Wire Railing Company (1857) and the Architectural Iron Works of the City of New York (1865). The term "lintel" more properly refers to a structural member, but this usage was evidently accepted during the 19th century. These ornaments, also called window mouldings, window heads, and window caps, are usually found on commercial buildings. Intended to imitate stone, they are often the chief decoration on upper floors of otherwise simple brick structures. A building contract of October 26, 1860, for a commercial structure at the corner of Royal and Customhouse Streets, specifies "20 semicircular ornamented window heads shall be furnished and set of cast iron for the 2nd and 3rd floors Front Windows. 10 square formed handsomely moulded and finished Cast Iron Window heads for 4th Story Front Windows." The repetition of the same patterns in several catalogs indicates that lintels were available in stock designs. Many window lintels reflect the Italianate style while others incorporate naturalistic designs, faces, and Classical motifs such as the egg and dart. The Leeds Store and Warehouse, designed by James Gallier, Jr., has two varieties of lintels in the Gothic style, evidently designed especially for this building. Such ornamented windows often have decorative cast-iron sills.

316 Magazine Street.

Private Residence.

From *Designs of Ornamental Ironwork* (1860-61).

The durability, strength, and reasonable price of cast iron made popular its use for exterior architectural elements such as columns and capitals. By the mid-19th century slender cast-iron columns were used to support verandahs. These columns were more resistant to weathering than wood posts and could be purchased in a variety of designs, usually Classical in derivation. Some columns have "post-collars," or rings of spikes, near the top designed to prevent intruders from climbing onto the verandahs. Large elaborate column capitals and pilaster capitals on fine homes and public buildings, formerly hand-carved of wood, were replaced by similar cast-iron elements. The decorative motifs of the capital could be cast in sections, then bolted on a tubular cast-iron sleeve, creating a cheaper and more durable capital. Other capitals were cast entirely in iron. Several have been located in the New Orleans area marked with the name of a New York firm, J. L. Jackson and Co. A number of New Orleans firms advertised their ability to provide columns or capitals: Wood, Miltenberger & Co., Luther Homes, Bennett & Lurges, Leeds & Co., and the Shakespeare Iron Foundry. In a building contract of June 4, 1851, with Horace Claiborne Cammack, President of the Saint Charles Hotel Company, the firm Homes & Bennett agreed to supply "...all the wrought and Cast Iron work of every description whatsoever plain ornamental or otherwise, required to complete the building." Included were "Corinthian Capitals and Bases for the Portico and Collonnade [sic], the Pilaster capitals & bases of the exterior" and "Ionic and Doric fluted columns with their caps and bases." Evidently Homes & Bennett ordered some capitals from the New York Wire Railing Company. The 1857 catalog of this firm contains two designs, numbers 514 and 515, for "Corregio Capitals. - Made for the Saint Charles Hotel, New Orleans."

1780 Prytania Street. 400 Tchoupitoulas Street.

3338 St. Charles Avenue.

Private Residence.

Corner Fourth and Chestnut Streets.

From *The Builder's Guide* (1850).

As the popularity of cast iron as a building material increased, foundries began to produce a greater variety of architectural elements. By mid-century, almost every element, formerly made of wood or wrought iron, was being manufactured: tie-ends, stairs, rosettes, cornices, ventilators, hardware, downspout boots. These were available in different designs and builders could choose combinations to suit their taste. They were decorative, inexpensive, and durable. Highly resistant to weathering if kept painted, cast-iron elements were favored for many exterior details. Interior cast-iron elements, such as ceiling centerpieces, were sometimes used in place of plaster or wood details. Cast-iron fireplace fronts and mantels were widely advertised. The mantels could be marbled, in imitation of the more expensive material, to give a richer appearance to the room.

From *Designs of Ornamental Ironwork* (1860-61).

1448 Prytania Street.

2228 St. Charles Avenue.

In 1858 the New Orleans representative of the Philadelphia firm, Wood & Perot, advertised the availability of "50 patterns of High Fences." By the last quarter of the 19th century, several firms specialized in the manufacture of fences. An 1895 advertisement of Hinderer's Iron Fence Works boasts "Iron Fences cheaper than wood." The fences produced earlier in the century are generally heavier, rich in design, and often surround large homes. Posts could be purchased in a variety of styles and combined with different railing patterns, sometimes identical to those on verandahs. The enormous posts at either side of a gate were either cast in their entirety or composed of decorative plates bolted together and reinforced with rods. Some fences bear the mark of Wood, Miltenberger & Co. and closely match designs found in the catalog of Wood & Perot. The most famous of New Orleans fences, the cornstalk design, was sold by this firm. Later fences, especially those surrounding cottages, are generally small and composed of bars joined by cast-iron decorative details. Many of these bear plates or marks attesting to their local origin: Chas. Pike, Hinderer's Iron Fence Works, Timpe & Spitz, and Lorio.

St. Louis Cemetery III.

St. Louis Cemetery III.

Cypress Grove Cemetery.

From *The Builder's Guide* (1850).

Cast-iron fences surrounding tombs are often identical to those enclosing yards, and bear maker's marks indicating their common origin. In cemeteries, extensive use was made of verandah railing patterns, sometimes accented by decorative motifs added to the top rail. Gates of cemetery fences, however, often differ from those found elsewhere, sometimes incorporating the name of the deceased and his date of death. Particular symbols of death are usually seen only in cemeteries, though in a few cases, gates of this type appear in residential areas. Frequently used designs are angels, weeping willows, inverted torches, and lambs.

A number of cast-iron tombs remain in New Orleans cemeteries, but were evidently not as popular as granite or marble structures. Some are unique and were probably designed especially for the client. A greater percentage can be seen in various locations, indicating that they were stock designs. Two of the finest tombs were built for New Orleans iron founders and were probably designed and cast in their foundries. One is the Leeds' tomb in Cypress Grove Cemetery. B. T. K. Bennett and James D. Edwards, proprietors of competing foundries, are interred in a single Gothic style tomb in Greenwood Cemetery. C. A. Miltenberger, also in the iron trade, is interred in a tomb identical to that of J. M. Pelton, nearby in Greenwood Cemetery. The Pelton tomb is marked "Robert Wood & Co., Philadelphia." Wood, Miltenberger & Co. advertise the availability of "Cast-Iron Mausoleums of beautiful design and finish," and a number of tombs bear their mark.

Edwards and Bennett tomb, Greenwood Cemetery.

Miltenberger tomb, Greenwood Cemetery.

Leeds tomb, Cypress Grove Cemetery.

From *Designs of Ornamental Ironwork* (1860-61).

During the 1850s, cast-iron garden furniture, fountains, and ornaments became increasingly popular. The furniture was produced in naturalistic patterns, such as the morning glory and rustic, in geometric patterns, and in designs incorporating motifs reflecting the popular furniture styles of the period. Some garden furniture exhibits Gothic details, other pieces have cabriole legs in the "French" manner, while furniture of the 1870s and 1880s reflects the linear designs of Charles Eastlake. Many fountains were produced, some Classical in detailing, which incorporated cupids or figures into their design. Cast-iron dogs, stags, rabbits, and urns were purchased to ornament gardens and cemeteries. The Wood & Perot catalog shows twenty-six designs for fountains and thirty for statuary. Most furniture and statuary in New Orleans was probably imported from centers of the trade. Local firms do not advertise their ability to manufacture these ornaments, though they may have produced some. Most pieces examined are marked with the names of New York and Philadelphia firms. Several chairs in Greenwood Cemetery, however, are marked "Hinderer's."

Greenwood Cemetery.

LEEDS' FOUNDRY,

ESTABLISHED IN 1825.

CORNER DELORD and CONSTANCE STS.,
NEW ORLEANS, LA.

WE ARE PREPARED TO MANUFACTURE

Sugar Mills, Steam Engines, Boilers, Sugar Kettles,

VACUUM PANS, DOUBLE AND TRIPLE EFFECTS,

Centrifugals, Draining Machines, Cotton Compresses, Furnace Mouths, Grate Bars, and all kinds of work for Sugar, Cotton and Rice Plantations, Steamboats and Steamships.

—WE ALSO MANUFACTURE—

McDonald's Automatic Hydraulic Pressure Regulators,
By which a constant pressure is kept up on the Mill, of which there are now over 100 in successful operation in this State, and

MITCHELL'S PATENT ROLLER ROUGHENER.
By which the Roller can be kept roughened during the grinding season. We are prepared to furnish to steam users,

THE COOK & THOEN'S
Feed : Water : Regulator!

Which fills a long felt want, and protects steam boilers against the dangers of

LOW WATER,

as the safety valve protects them against over pressure. It automatically regulates the speed of a boiler feeder, according to the height of the water in the boiler. If more water is evaporated in the boiler, the boiler feeder runs faster, and slower if less water is evaporated, whereby a uniform water level in the boiler is maintained at all times.

—ALSO THE—

THOEN'S STEAM TRAP
For the discharge of Condensed Water.

LEEDS & CO., LIMITED.

Orders left at Box 96, Mechanics'. Dealers' and Lumbermen's Exchange, will receive prompt attention.

From *Wilkinson's Report* (1890).

San Francisco Plantation.

The manufacture of heavy machinery supported the decorative cast-iron industry in New Orleans. Some large firms advertised their ability to produce sugar mill equipment and steam engines, adding parenthetically that they produced architectural elements. One such firm, Leeds & Co., whose success was based on sugar mill equipment, cast several building fronts during the mid-19th century and undoubtedly produced other architectural elements. Wood, Miltenberger & Co., Luther Homes, and Bennett & Lurges seem to have been the only large foundries specializing in the manufacture of architectural elements. John Armstrong's Foundry and Boiler Manufactory, Reynolds Iron Works, Shakspeare Iron Foundry, and other firms apparently combined the production of architectural elements with their primary business of producing marine equipment, saw mills, railroad and steam engines, etc. Other large firms, such as Whitney Iron Works, Edwards Iron Works, and Johnson Iron Works, advertised only that they produced machinery, although they may have manufactured some architectural elements.

47

800 Royal Street.

2825-2829 Constance Street.

SOME NEW ORLEANS INDIVIDUALS AND FIRMS SPECIALIZING IN ORNAMENTAL IRONWORK

This list is a compilation of facts derived from city directories, newspapers, death notices, and guides to the city. The dates represent specific listings found for the firms. Because of conflicting information in 19th century sources, it was difficult to determine precisely the years a business was in operation.

JOHN ARMSTRONG

Foundry & Boiler Manufactory, cor. Suzette and New Levee. 1855. Cor. Erato and New Levee. 1857, 1858, 1861. Erato near Peters St. 1870, 1871.
Armstrong advertised machinery and "Iron Columns and fronts for buildings, ventilators, sash weights, railings, etc." His residence is listed as "N.W. cor. of Carondelet and Washington". The house has a fine verandah, possibly cast in his foundry. A native of Ireland, he died in 1870.

JACOB BAUMILLER

Hoist wheel manufacturer, 21 St. Joseph St. 1846. Baumiller & Goodwyn, Hoist wheels, Builders' Ironwork, 1 Carroll St. 1851.
"Manufacturer of iron verandahs, balconies, office railings... builders' work in general; hoist wheels and derrick machines." 7 Carroll St. 1857, 1858, 1859, 1860, 1861, 1866, 1870. 293 Dryades St. 1880.
Baumiller's house smithing commissions included the ironwork for the J. C. Morris home at First and Coliseum Streets. He also added a verandah cast in Cincinnati and "Baumiller & Goodwyn's dental cornice" to a building at the southwest corner of South and Camp Streets. Baumiller, a native of Pennsylvania, died January 11,1887.

BENJAMIN T. K. BENNETT AND FRANCIS LURGES

Bennett & Co., New Orleans Ornamental Iron Works, 55, 57 Circus St. 1856, 1857. 101 Rampart St. 1858.
Bennett and Lurges (Francis Lurges), New Orleans Ornamental Iron Works, 55, 57 Circus St. 1859.
Bennett & Lurges, Foundry, Magnolia and Erato Sts.; Office, 116 Carondelet St. 1860, 1861.
New Orleans Ornamental Iron Works (Estate of Francis Lurges), same foundry location with office at 118 Carondelet. 1870.

Both Bennett & Co. and Bennett & Lurges advertised architectural elements with no mention of machinery. 1857 is the first listing for Bennett & Lurges with a foundry location in their business address. This firm cast the front for the Bank of America building designed by James Gallier, Jr. Francis Lurges died in 1869. Bennett died before 1874, according to his wife's obituary, and is buried in a cast-iron tomb in Greenwood Cemetery.

WILLIS P. AND H. DUDLEY COLEMAN

Coleman's Patent Undulatory Mills (W. P. Coleman, Inventor and Manufacturer),
City office: 97 Tchoupitoulas St. 1851. Manufactory: Kenner, La. (New Orleans Office) St. Charles St. opp. Commercial Alley. 1859.
H. Dudley Coleman & Bro., 9 Perdido St. 1868, 1879.
H. Dudley Coleman, Foundry and Plantation Machinery, Square of Magnolia, Erato, Clio, and Clara Sts. (Purchase of Bennett & Lurges' Foundry); office, 9 Perdido St. 1882.

H. Dudley Coleman Machinery Co., Ltd., same address. 1894, 1899. Coleman advertised the manufacture of machinery and, according to a *Sunday States* article (1887), had contracts for architectural work, including D. Mercier's Sons at Canal and Dauphine Streets. H. D. Coleman was a financial and civic leader, elected Representative to Congress in 1888. He died in 1926 in Biloxi.

WILLIAM EBERT

Foreman, Southern Ornamental Iron Works (Wood, Miltenberger & Co.) 1870. "Ornamental Iron Works and General House Smithing...," 129 and 131 Magazine St. 1872, 1876.
William Ebert (successor to Wood, Miltenberger & Co., Southern Ornamental Iron Works), Ornamental Iron & Wire Works, 194 Magazine St. 1879, 1880, 1882.
Ebert Architectural Iron Works, McConneghy & O'Connor, Proprs. 1885, 1886.
Ebert Architectural Iron Works, O'Connor and Reynolds, Proprs., 103 and 107 Julia St. 1888.
Mr. Ebert, born in Germany, died October 10, 1885, in New Orleans.

CARL A. FREDERICK HINDERER

Hinderer and Daimler, 304 Camp Street. 1886. (listed with furniture dealers)
Hinderer's Iron Fence Works, Camp St. opp. the Margaret Monument. 1894, 1895. Also called the Novelty Iron & Fence Works.
Hinderer's specialties were railings, fences, garden ornaments, and furniture. Carl Hinderer, an exile from Germany, died in 1910.

LUTHER HOMES

Luther Homes, Blacksmith. 1846.
Homes & Bennett, "Manufacturers of the latest and most approved style of iron railings, verandahs, door vaults, etc.," 104, 106 St. Charles St. 1846, 1852, 1853, 1854.
Luther Homes, Foundry and Ornamental Iron Works (successor to Homes & Bennett), Foundry, Benton and Euphrosine Sts.; office, 106 St. Charles St. 1852, 1857, 1858, 1860, 1861.
Luther Homes, Sec. and Treas. of the Mechanic's Agricultural Fair Association.
Office: Mechanic's Institute, Dryades St.; Foundry: cor. Franklin and Euphrosine St. 1867.
Luther Homes was Recording Secretary for the Mechanic's Society in 1870 and Librarian in 1880.
Homes & Bennett, according to a building contract of 1851, was commissioned to do the ironwork for the new St. Charles Hotel. A native of Massachusetts, Luther Homes died July 11, 1881.

JEDEDIAH AND CHARLES J. LEEDS

Jedediah Leeds, Leeds & Co. (Established 1825), 86 Delord St. 1838.
Jno., Chas. & Thos. Leeds, Iron Foundry, cor. Foucher and Delord. 1846, 1850,
1856, 1857, 1858, 1861, 1868, 1869.
Chas. J., Jno., Mrs. T. L. Leeds, (Mrs. E. Grinnell), Manufacturers of Vertical and Horizontal Steam Engines, etc. 1870.
Leeds & Co., Manufacturers of all machinery required for the South, Constance and Delord St. 1880, 1885.
Leeds & Co., Ltd., Foundry & Machine Works, Delord, Constance, Tchoupitoulas, and St. Joseph Sts. Charles J. Leeds, Pres. 1894. Foundry and office: cor. Howard Ave. (late Delord) and Constance St., Tel. 1541. 1895.
Possibly the largest and most technologically advanced foundry in New Orleans, Leeds manufactured both machinery and builders' ironwork. Leeds & Co.'s foundry cast the iron columns for the Treme Market in 1839. They also cast the building front for the

New Orleans Savings Institution, 1873, at the corner of Canal and Baronne. In 1885 Leeds & Co. smelted Louisiana iron ore and produced Louisiana pig iron. Charles J. Leeds, the founder's son, was an important business and community leader who was elected Mayor of New Orleans in 1874. He died in 1898.

C. A. MILTENBERGER

Wood, Miltenberger & Co., 101 Gravier St. March 1, 1858. (announcement of association between Chas. A. Miltenberger, New Orleans, Robt. Wood, Philadelphia, and Elliston Perot, Philadelphia)
Wood, Miltenberger & Co., Southern Ornamental Iron Works (Wood & Perot, Philadelphia), Wareroom, 57 Camp St. Foundry and Machine Shop, No. 247 Tchoupitoulas St. 1858, 1859, 1860, 1861.
C. A. Miltenberger, Coal Commission Merchant, 57 Camp St. 1866. Southern Ornamental Iron Works, C. A. Miltenberger, Propr., 194 Magazine, office 53 Camp. 1870.
Wm. Ebert (successor to Miltenberger). 1872, 1880. (see Ebert)

Comparison of marked ornamental ironwork in New Orleans indicates that the work of Wood, Miltenberger & Co. was exceptional in pattern and craftsmanship.

WILLIAM H. REYNOLDS

Crescent Iron Works, W. H. Reynolds, Propr., 223, 225, 227 Front, "Prepared to make contracts for wrought ironwork...Carey's Patent Earth Borers." 1870.
Reynolds Iron Works, bet. Fulton and Water, S. Market and Delord. 1882, 1887, 1888. Cor. Fulton and Delord. 1888, 1894.
Reynolds Iron Works Co., Ltd., bet. Fulton and S. Water St., S. Diamond and Howard Ave., Tel. 923. 1895.

Machinery, builders' ironwork for the Rice-Born Hardware Co. Building, the Grand Opera House on Canal St., and Timpe's Patent Elevators were among the products of Reynolds Iron Works. The building at 218 Camp Street, presently occupied by the Junior Achievement of New Orleans, Inc., bears the mark of Reynolds Iron Works. Mr. Reynolds, a native of New Orleans, died in 1917.

SAMUEL AND JOSEPH SHAKSPEARE

Shakspeare, blacksmith, Triton Walk, b. Apollo and Bacchus. 1838.
Samuel Shakspeare, blacksmith, 194 Julia St. 1846.
Wheeler, Geddes & Co., 208 Girod St. 1860.
Geddes, Shakspeare & Co., 208 Girod, bet. Baronne and Dryades St. 1861, 1868, 1869, 1870.
Shakspeare, Smith & Co., office, 219 Girod St. 1880, 1885, 1887, 1892, 1894. Shakspeare & Swoop, 913 Girod, near Baronne, Tel. 54. 1895. Julian M. Swoop, Propr., Shakspeare Iron Works. 1899.
A *Daily States* (1887) article mentions that the Shakspeare foundry was manufacturing both machinery, such as rice mills, for the country parishes and all the architectural ironwork for the store of I. L. Lyons & Co. on the corner of Camp and Gravier St. The sugar machinery trade was enlarged by Mr. Swoop, propr., in 1902. *(Daily Crescent,* 1903) Joseph Shakspeare is well-known for his work when he was elected Mayor of New Orleans, in 1880 and again in 1882, and for his contribution to industry.

IRONWORKING BUSINESSES

The following firms were listed in city directories or placed advertisements in newspapers in the years shown. This list does not reflect all the years a firm was in operation and should serve only as a beginning for further research. The list illustrates the number and diversity of businesses involved in iron working in New Orleans.

ALGIERS IRON WORKS CO., LTD., Algiers. 1894.

BARONNE STREET STEAM BOILER MANUFACTORY, bet. Poydras and Hevia St. 1860.

M. BASTIAN, IRON BEDSTEAD MANUFACTORY, Girod St. near Baronne. 1859, 1861.

WM. A. BEECHER, STEAM RAILING WORKS, 48 Chartres St. 1849.

BLACK AND HOLLY, IRON WORKERS, 110 Poydras St. 1859.

H. N. BOUDET & CO., WIRE WORKS & STEAM BIRD CAGE FACTORY, RAILINGS, ETC., 105 St. Charles St. 1885.

BREWSTER, BLAKENEY & CO., COPPERSMITHS AND SHEET IRON WORKERS. 1860. Front and Fulton St. bet. Julia and Notre Dame. 1861.

BROOKS, PURSEGLOVE, IRON FOUNDERS, Carrollton. 1861.

CHRISTIE & CORNWELL, IRON RAILING MANUFACTORY, 323 Rampart St. 1858.

J. CHRISTIE, IRON FOUNDER, 323 Rampart. 1861.

JOHN CLARK, IRON & BRASS FOUNDRY & BOILER MANUFACTORY, cor. Tchoupitoulas and Race St. 1861, 1875.

COCHRAN & MIMS, ENGINEERS, MACHINISTS, BRASS & IRON FOUNDERS, 292, 294 Peters and 306 Tchoupitoulas St. 1882. 296-312 S. Peters St. 1888.

COLTON & BALDWIN, COPPER, TIN AND SHEET IRON WORKERS, 10 Canal St. and 9 Crossman St. 1860, 1861.

J. D. CONNELL & GEORGE E. RATHBURN, ENGINEERS AND BOILERMAKERS, 1027 S. Peters. 1898.

COOK & FALLON, BELLEVILLE IRON WORKS, Algiers. 1857, 1858, 1859.

CRESCENT CITY CORNICE WORKS, BACKUS AND BRISKIN, 247-251 Magazine St. 1885.

CRESCENT CITY CORNICE AND ORNAMENTAL WORKS, R. A. VANCLEAVE, JR. (Successor to this branch of Daniel Edwards' Iron Works), 247-251 Magazine St.

GEORGE CRONAN, SOUTHERN ORNAMENTAL IRON WORKS (Successor to Bennett & Lurges), cor. Magnolia and Erato Sts. 1871.

L. F. DELAMARE, ZINC, COPPER, TIN & SHEET IRON MANUFACTORY, 57 Franklin St., bet. Conti and Bienville. 1849.

S. DILLER, FOUNDRY, St. Thomas n. Annunciation. 1858.

DONALD & McKENZIE, BOILERMAKERS, BLACKSMITHS, & MARINE WORK, 119, 121 Front St. and 112, 114 Fulton. 1885.

EDWARDS (Family) IRON WORKS (Daniel, James D. and Daniel). 1855-1895. Daniel Edwards, a native of Liverpool, began his business as a tin, copper and sheet iron works; later, the specialty of machinery founding was developed.

EICHORN & LESTER, COPPER, TIN, SHEET IRON & CORNICE WORKERS.

J. FAIVRE, MANUFACTURER OF PIANOFORTES AND INVENTOR OF THE IRON FRAME PIANO, 46 late 56 Royal St. 1861.

P. FINNEGAN, COPPERSMITH, SHEET IRON WORKER, 665 Magazine St. 1880.

GALWAY & DUFFY, ST. LOUIS STREET FOUNDRY. 1880.

RIVIERE GARDERES' "PHOENIX" FOUNDRY, 39 Exchange Place. 1857, 1858, 1861.

LOUIS GILLET & PIERRE CAMET, IRON FOUNDERS, 275 St. Philip. 1827.

GILLETTE–HERZOG MANUFACTURING CO., STRUCTURAL IRON AND STEEL SPECIFICATIONS. 1895.

M. GOLDEN, IRON VERANDAHS, ETC., Delord cor. Baronne. 1858.

HALLER & BRO., COPPER, TIN, & SHEET IRON WORKERS, 247 Tchoupitoulas. 1858, 1861.

ELEAZAR HOLMES, IRON FOUNDER, 58 Delord. 1827.

LEWIS JOHNSON, IRON AND BRASS FOUNDER, cor. Front and Julia Sts. 1871. Julia from Delta to S. Water St., P.O. Box 2234. 1880.

JOHNSON IRON WORKS CO., LTD., Julia from Delta to S. Water Sts. 1894, 1895, 1899.

JULIA STREET FOUNDRY, 200 Julia St. 1851.

LAWRENCE KEARNS, BOILER MAKER, Julia St. bet. Tchoupitoulas and New Levee. 1854.

KILLEEN'S FOUNDRY AND IRON WORKS, 275 St. Louis St. 1887. Liberty bet. Girod and Julia Sts., Tel. 1194. 1899.

KURSHEEDT & BIENVENU, BUILDERS' HARDWARE, MANTELS, MONUMENTS, TOMBS, 114, 120, 122 Camp St. 1885.

NUMA J. LORIO, IRON AND FENCEWORKS, 1051-53 Camp, Tel. Main 1047. 1913, 1914.

LOUISIANA FOUNDRY, New Levee St. bet. Delord and Calliope. 1861.

LOUISIANA MANUFACTURING & COOPERAGE CO., P. Hirsch, President, St. Louis bet. N. Tonti and N. Rocheblave. 1895.

LOUISIANA MATTRESS, IRON & SPRING BED CO., LTD., J. Boyle, President, 411-413 S. Front St. 1895.

J. MAURY, BUILDERS IRON WORKS, VERANDAHS, ETC., Hospital cor. Burgundy. 1857, 1858, 1861.

McCAN & HARRELL, IRON FOUNDERS, Fulton n. Notre Dame. 1861.

McCAN & PATTERSON, FOUNDRY & MACHINE SHOP, cor. Delord and New Levee. 1858.

D. C. McCAN, IRON & BRASS FOUNDER, Fulton, New Levee, Notre Dame and Julia Sts. 1871, 1899.

CAPT. JOHN McLEAN, IRON FOUNDER, 489 Old Levee. 1861.

M. A. MORSE, JR., IRON WORKER, Algiers. 1899.

JOHN H. MURPHY, COPPER, BRASS & IRON WORKS, Magazine St. 1886, 1895, 1899. (Boiler Works, Broad, Poydras and Dorgenois St. 1899.)

NEW ORLEANS IRON FOUNDRY, T. VAURIGAUD, Levee bet. Montegut and Clouet Sts. 1838.

NEW ORLEANS TYPE FOUNDRY, 66 Gravier St. 1860.

NOVELTY IRON WORKS, Cor. Peters and Delord St. 1882.

JAMES NUTTALL, HOUSE SMITH, BELL HANGER, RAILINGS, ETC. 1858, 1859.

ORLEANS FOUNDRY, ARTHUR THOMPSON, 6-8 St. Ferdinand St. 1838, 1859.

ORLEANS ORNAMENTAL IRON & FENCE WORKS, HAMMOND, TIMPE, & SPITZ, Dryades cor. Jackson Ave. 1895.

ORLEANS ORNAMENTAL IRON & FENCE WORKS, TIMPE & SPITZ, 2222 Dryades. 1898.

J. T. OSBORN, MANUFACTURER OF COPPER, TIN & SHEET IRON, BLACKSMITH, 126 New Levee St. 1837.

GEORGE PATTERSON, FOUNDRY & MACHINE SHOP (Successor to McCan & Patterson), cor. Delord and New Levee. 1859, 1860.

PIERRE PELANNE, BLACKSMITH & IRON FENCE BUILDER (Bros. Pelanne), 39 St. Philip. 1859, 1861.

PHOENIX FOUNDRY, Gretna, La. 1848, 1851, 1857, 1858.

CHARLES A. PIKE, Foreman W. Ebert. 1880.

C. PIKE, IRON FENCE WORKS, cor. Julia and Magazine Sts. 1892, 1894, 1895.

DANIEL PIKE, PROPR., LOUISIANA ORNAMENTAL IRON & FENCE WORKS, 1024 St. Charles Ave. 1895.

SCHWARTZ FOUNDRY, MANUFACTURERS OF SUGAR MACHINERY (Successors to Leeds & Co.), cor. Howard and Constance, Long Distance Tel. 525. 1896, 1899.

J. SIMONDS & CO., COPPER, TIN & SHEET IRON WORKERS, cor. Customhouse and Levee Sts. 1885.

SOUTHERN PLATING & WIRE WORKS (Successor to Boudet & Co.), St. Charles St. 1888, 1895.

JOSEPH SUTTON & SON, IRON FOUNDERS (Successor to Cochran & Mims), S. Peters near Erato. 1894, 1899.

P. THELEN, MACHINIST & BRASS FOUNDER, 104 Tchoupitoulas St. 1894, 1895.

JEAN THIAC, IRON FOUNDER, 174 Levee St. 1827.

JOHN WARD, STEAM BOILER MANUFACTURER, 262 Tchoupitoulas St. 1860.

WHITNEY IRON WORKS, CO., Tchoupitoulas at St. Joseph and Foucher Sts. 1883, 1885; 1896.

W. K. WILSON, COPPER, BRASS & SHEET IRON WORKER, 169-171 Tchoupitoulas St. (New numbers 827, 829). 1894.

BIBLIOGRAPHY

19TH CENTURY SOURCES

The Art Journal Illustrated Catalogue of the International Exhibition. The Art Journal. London and New York: James S. Virtue, 1862.

Benjamin, Asher. *The Builder's Guide or Complete System of Architecture.* Boston: Benjamin B. Mussey & Co., 1860.

Brice, Wallace A. *New Orleans Merchant's Diary and Guide for 1867-68.* Vol. I. New Orleans: Wharton, 1857.

Cohen's New Orleans City Directory for 1855. *New Orleans: Cohen. 1865.*

Constitution. By-Laws, and Rules of Order of the New Orleans Mechanic Society. The New Orleans Mechanic Society. New Orleans: Price Current Offices, Printers, 1855.

Crescent City Business Directory for 1858-59. Compiled by Price Current Newspaper Offices. New Orleans: Price Current Offices, 1858.

The Crystal Palace Exhibition. Illustrated Catalogue (London, 1851) Reprint, with a new introduction by John Gloag. New York: Dover Publications, Inc., 1970.

Descriptive Catalogue of the Manufactures of the New York Wire Railing Company. *Hutchinson and Wickersham. New York: Fowler & Wells, 1857.*

Designs of Ornamental Ironwork. Robert Wood & Co. Philadelphia: Robert Wood & Co.. 1860-61 (dates of plates).

Edwards, Richard. *Edwards' Annual Directory of New Orleans and Suburbs.* New Orleans: Southern Publishing Co., 1870.

Emaillerie & Ateliers de Construction de Dietrich & Cie, Niederbronn. (Alsace), 3e Partie. Paris: 37 Blvd. Magenta. Strasbourg: 1 Quai Kleber, ler Janvier, 1882.

Fairbairn, William. *Iron: Its History, Properties and the Process of Manufacture.* New Edition, Revised and Enlarged. Edinburgh: Adam and Charles Black, 1865.

Fairbairn, William. On the Application of Cast and Wrought Iron to Building Purposes. *New York: John Wiley, 1854.*

Fonte de Fer. A. Durenne, Maitre des Forges. Paris: A. Durenne, no date.

Forbes, C. W., Compiler. Handbook of the Mechanics' Dealers' and Lumbermens' Exchange. *New Orleans: Forbes, 1892.*

Freedley, Edwin T. *Philadelphia and its Manufactures: A Handbook.* Exhibiting the Development, Variety, and Statistics of the Manufacturing Industry of Philadelphia in 1857. Philadelphia: Edward Young, 1858.

Gardner, Charles. Gardner's New Orleans City Directory for 1861. New Orleans: Gardner, 1861.

Gardner, Chas. *Gardner & Wharton's New Orleans Directory, for 1869.* Including Jefferson City, Gretna, Carrollton, Algiers, McDonough. New Orleans: Gardner, 1859.

Gibson, John. *Gibson's Guide and Directory of the State of Louisiana and the Cities of New Orleans and Lafayette.* New Orleans: Gibson, 1838.

Graham, L., Compiler. *Graham and Madden's Crescent City Directory for 1870.* Including Jefferson City, Carrollton, Algiers, Gretna & Milneburg (Title page missing). New Orleans: L.Graham, 1870.

Jewell, Edwin L., Editor and Compiler. *Crescent City, Illustrated.* New Orleans: Jewell, 1873.

Kirk, Edward, Et. Al. *The Founding of Metals.* A Practical Treatise on the Melting of Iron, etc. 5th Edition. New York: David Williams, 1885.

Land, John E. *Penn Illustrations of New Orleans, 1881-2.* New Orleans: Jno. E. Land, 1882.

Morrison, Andrew, Compiler and Editor. *New Orleans and the New South.* New Orleans: Graham, 1888.

Morrison, Andrew. *The Industries of New Orleans.* New Orleans: J. M. Elstner and Co., 1885.

Mygatt, A. & Co. *New Orleans Business Directory.* Also a business directory of Algiers, Baton Rouge, Natchez, Vicksburg, Bayou Sara, Clinton, & Port Hudson. With a map, comp. and arr. by W. H. Rainey (map missing). New Orleans, La.: Mygatt, 1857.

New Orleans: The Crescent City. The book of the Chamber of Commerce and Industry of Louisiana, and other public bodies of the Crescent City. New Orleans: George W. Engelhardt, 1894.

Norman, Benjamin Moore. *New Orleans and Its Environs.* New York: D. Appleton and Co., 1845.

Phoenix Iron Works. George S. Lincoln & Co. Hartford, Connecticut: George S. Lincoln & Co., 1853.

Soard, L. *Soard's New Orleans City Directory for 1880.* New Orleans: Soard's Publishing Co., 1880.

Soard, L. *Soard's New Orleans City Directory for 1895*. New Orleans: Soard's Publishing Co., 1895.

Soard, L. *Soard's New Orleans City Directory for 1914*. New Orleans: Soard's Publishing Co., 1914.

Spretson, N. E., Engineer. *A Practical Treatise on Casting and Founding.* Including descriptions of modern machinery employed in the art. 6th Edition. London, New York: E. & F. N. Spon, 1892.

Waldo, J. Curtis. *Illustrated Visitor's Guide to New Orleans*. New Orleans: J. Curtis Waldo, 1879.

West, Thomas D. *American Foundry Practice.* Treating of Loam, Dry Sand and Green Sand Moulding and Containing a Practical Treatise upon the Management of Cupolas and the Melting of Iron. 5th Edition, Rev. New York: John Wiley & Sons, 1885.

Wilkinson, J. B., Jr. Wilkinson's Report on Diffusion and Mill Work in the Louisiana Sugar Harvest of 1889-'90. New Orleans: J.B. Wilkinson, Jr., 1890.

NEWSPAPERS

L'Abeille de la Nouvelle Orleans.
Commercial Bulletin (New Orleans).
Daily Crescent (New Orleans).
Daily Delta (New Orleans).
Daily Picayune (New Orleans).
Daily States (New Orleans).
Deutsche Zeitung (New Orleans).
Le Courrier de la Louisiane (New Orleans).
Le Sucrier de la Louisiane (Iberia).
Louisiana State Republican (New Orleans).
New Orleans Republican.
Southern Traveller (City of Lafayette in Jefferson Parish and town of Carrollton).
Sugar Bowl and Farm Journal (Iberia).
Sugar Planter's Journal (West Baton Rouge).
Sunday Picayune (New Orleans).
Taglische Deutsche Zeitung (New Orleans).

Times-Democrat and Daily Picayune (New Orleans).
Times-Picayune (New Orleans).
Weekly Delta (Monday Edition of *Daily Delta,* New Orleans).

Notarial Archives. City of New Orleans, records of E. Barnett, T. Beck, R. Brennan, H. P. Caire, L. T. Caire, H. B. Cenas, J. Cuvillier, and A. Mazureau concerning building contracts.

THE LOUISIANA LANDMARKS SOCIETY

The Louisiana Landmarks Society was established in 1950. However, its historic preservation advocacy activities began at the start of 1949 when members of the formative New Orleans chapter of the Society of Architectural Historians (an outgrowth of a history of Louisiana architecture course taught at Tulane University by Samuel Wilson, Jr.) banded together to save an early-nineteenth-century colonial Creole plantation, called the David Olivier House, from demolition. Leading the charge to preserve Gallier Hall in the 1950s and defeat the proposed Riverfront Expressway in the 1960s, Landmarks rapidly defined preservation advocacy in New Orleans. The current mission of the Louisiana Landmarks Society, the city and state's first historic preservation organization, is to promote historic preservation through education, advocacy, and operation of the Pitot House.

The values of the Louisiana Landmarks Society are manifested in the Pitot House, the nonprofit organization's home since 1964. This rare surviving example of colonial-era Creole architecture provides Landmarks with a site for exhibitions and educational programming that promote its preservation message. The historic structure and its interpreted grounds provide a transformative historic house tour experience for local and out-of-town visitors and provide the local public with a historically authentic and aesthetically idyllic setting for private functions.

The Louisiana Landmarks Society's major programs include an annual series of free public lectures on preservation topics, award recognition for outstanding preservation efforts, and the presentation of New Orleans' Nine Most Endangered properties—a program modeled after the National Trust for Historic Preservation's Eleven Most Endangered program.

In 1987, the board of trustees of the Louisiana Landmarks Society established a publication fund, named in honor of Samuel Wilson, Jr. The object of Landmarks' publication activity is to foster a more general interest in the architectural tradition of the region and to encourage publication of regional architectural history research. In the years since, Landmarks has published and marketed numerous monographs on architecture and preservation topics. By 2010, efforts to expand Landmarks' publishing program resulted in the creation of a publishing and distribution partnership with Pelican Publishing Company. Landmarks' share of proceeds from this partnership will support perpetuation of the Samuel Wilson, Jr. Publication Fund and its mission to provide for the development of future Louisiana Landmarks Society publications.

www.ingramcontent.com/pod-product-compliance
Lightning Source LLC
Chambersburg PA
CBHW031657040426
42453CB00006B/335